Celebrating
Holy Week

Vincent Sherlock

First published in 2019 by Messenger Publications

The material in this publication is protected by copyright law. Except as may be permitted by law, no part of the material may be reproduced (including by storage in a retrieval system) or transmitted in any form or by any means, adapted, rented or lent without the written permission of the copyright owners. Applications for permissions should be addressed to the publisher.

The right of Vincent Sherlock to be identified as the author of the Work has been asserted by him in accordance with the Copyright and Related Rights Act, 2000.

ISBN: 978 1 78812 020 3

Copyright © Vincent Sherlock, 2019

Designed by Messenger Publications Design Department
Typeset in Times New Roman, Trajan Pro and Herculanem
Printed by Nicholson & Bass Ltd

Messenger Publications,
37 Lower Leeson Street, Dublin 2
www.messenger.ie

CONTENTS

INTRODUCTION ~ 1

PALM SUNDAY ~ 3

THE TRIDUUM ~ 7

HOLY THURSDAY ~ 10

GOOD FRIDAY ~ 16

HOLY SATURDAY ~ 23

THE EASTER VIGIL ~ 25

AN EASTER SUNDAY STORY ~ 31

CONCLUSION ~ 33

THEY WONDERED ~ 35

Introduction

My father, God rest him, had an accident many years ago and, as a result, lost the sight in one eye. In his later years, the sight in the other eye began to deteriorate. It was decided that he needed to have a cataract removed and the appointment was given for 7.45am on Good Friday. My niece and I took him to Sligo General for the procedure. It was a lovely morning, clear skies and all was well, but he told me he didn't know how I was able to drive in such an awful fog. This made me aware of what he was looking through. Though the day was perfectly clear, his view of it was through a heavy fog. There was no doubt he needed the surgery!

The procedure was relatively fast and simple and shortly after 9am he was ready to go home, but his eye was bandaged, and he was now completely blind and dependant on us. We guided him as best we could to the car, got him in and headed for home. I told him where we were along the way – Ballymote, Gurteen, Mullaghroe and home. We helped him from the car and took him to the sitting room. The fog of the morning was now total darkness for him. He spent the rest of Good Friday like that.

On Holy Saturday I went home. He was unbandaged but felt there was grit in his eye, and he was in some discomfort. He was okay but a bit down. He knew, as we all did, that there was always a slight possibility that things might not work out. It is possible that he was thinking of this on Saturday. We reassured him that he would improve and, though he agreed, he looked very vulnerable and was, I'm certain, more than a little worried.

On Easter Sunday morning, I got a text message from my brother – sent shortly after 7am. He had gone home and found my father at the kitchen table, sitting there and reading an old parish bulletin. Yes, reading and doing so without glasses. He told my brother he had weighed himself and was three pounds lighter than my niece had told him. He could see the scales. My brother's text concluded 'I hope I did not wake you, but this is good news!' So, it was and remains!

There seems to me to be a link in the move from Good Friday to Easter Sunday. My father's Good Friday began in a cloud, moved into darkness that lasted through Friday and Saturday. Easter Sunday morning brought new sight and light and, as my brother so rightly said, 'Good News'.

PALM SUNDAY

Before we move to The Triduum – the journey from Holy Thursday, through Good Friday and Holy Saturday and leading us to Easter Sunday and its emptied tomb, we need to spend a bit of time with Palm Sunday or as it is also called Passion Sunday.

This day recalled the entry of Jesus into Jerusalem and the lead into days that would see a shift in attitude that can all too easily happen when the individual gets lost in the crowd. On Palm Sunday, there were many individuals who looked to Jesus for salvation and saw in him, a truly wonderful person who brought healing where he travelled and who spoke to them 'with authority' – that did not mean control or condescension but rather the welcome authority of one who spoke with a voice that was reassuring because he knew who he was and his words came from that place of knowing.

There was clear evidence that there was something very special to be found by anyone who spent time with him. We recall the woman at the well and her conversion, the centurion who felt unworthy to have Jesus under his roof but knew that a word from him was enough – 'Say only the word and my servant shall be healed'. We remember the widow woman on the outskirts of Nain, in funeral procession going to bury her only child and Jesus reaching out to her. We hear again his calling the disciples, having first invited the first of them to 'come and see' where he lived. There was clear evidence that he was a good and noble man and many individuals in the crowd knew that. They went to see him as he entered the city on a borrowed colt and were glad to be there. Excitement ruled the day, branches were cut from trees and were laid on the ground with cloaks and clothing to herald his arrival. 'Hosanna' was shouted – total excitement and unbridled joy.

Yet within that group too, there were some who were hostile, and their voices were not to be silenced. They knew what the others knew but maybe a bit more too. They knew that he had the wherewithal to bring a lasting change and they were not ready for that. They were not ready to relent their power and the control they enjoyed. There was still a role for their power and domination and that role would play itself out in the coming days.

Negativity had its say. Jealousy had its hour and the individuals in the crowd lost courage as the voice of the crowd took centre stage. 'Hosanna' was to be replaced by 'crucify' and welcome gave way to hostility. The voice of the individual, the heart of the individual, was overtaken by the herd mentality of the crowd and the good word was lost. A known and feared criminal was set free and the innocent submitted to an unwarranted trial. The drama moved from city streets and public roads to courtrooms and palaces and decisions were made in places where the ordinary man or woman cannot freely travel.

These same decisions were filtered to the crowd by people whose motives were not well-intentioned and whose attitudes were flawed. By the time the word got to the individual, the crowd had taken control. The welcome of Palm Sunday was to be short-lived and the joy of the people, the ones who had looked forward to encountering Christ, gave way to or was overtaken by negativity, hostility, cruelty and cowardice.

Palm Sunday then stands as a reminder to us that he had to enter Jerusalem but also as a challenge to be committed to our faith to a point where we are not easily led down paths not of our making or choosing.

The days to follow, the days of Holy Week, will invite us to walk with him and with a crowd that may well be hostile towards him or unable to grasp his reality. We will experience, with Peter perhaps, that confusion that leads us to moments of denial and tears. We will find something of the reluctant Simon in us too, that doesn't necessarily want to be directly involved but is nonetheless. Hopefully we will find something as well of the loyalty of those women who accompanied him all the way and find, with the solider at the foot of the cross, our voice as we too acclaim, 'In truth, this man was a son of God'; or the 'Good Thief' whose prayer, 'Jesus, remember me when you come into your kingdom' was answered immediately and in full.

Notice that much of what we might term 'memorable and worthy' that we recall from this day and in the days to come centres on individuals finding their voice and being willing to encounter Jesus. Maybe that's where we need to locate ourselves too in the days ahead, as man, woman or child wanting to encounter the Lord and willing to let our voice be heard. Our voice joining with other voices, becoming congregation rather than 'crowd' and opting to be faithful rather than vindictive.

There's a lot of ground to be travelled this week and many words to be spoken and primary among them will be the cry of Good Friday: 'It is accomplished'.

THE TRIDUUM

On the first day of Unleavened Bread, when the Passover lamb was sacrificed, his disciples said to him, 'Where do you want us to go and make the preparations for you to eat the Passover?' So he sent two of his disciples, saying to them, 'Go into the city and you will meet a man carrying a pitcher of water. Follow him, and say to the owner of the house that he enters, "The Master says: Where is my dining room in which I can eat the Passover with my disciples?" He will show you a large upper room furnished with couches, all prepared. Make the preparations for us there.' The disciples set out and went to the city and found everything as he had told them and prepared the Passover. (Mk 14:12–16)

There is something very special about this short passage from Mark's Gospel. A lot being said in a few lines and maybe that's what makes it special.

Jesus, it seems to me, lived his life in borrowed places. Born in a borrowed stable, early life lived in a borrowed country, hospitality borrowed from people like Martha, Mary and Lazarus, Passover meal in a borrowed room and death saw him rest in a borrowed tomb. As we reflect on Holy Week, could it be the case he wants to borrow something from you? Something precious and totally your gift to share with him? I think so. He is borrowing not anything you have but all that you are. He is borrowing you! Borrowing you, that like the stable, the foreign country, the friends' home, the Upper Room and the tomb, he may bring something of himself to you in these most sacred days.

Holy Week, central to all our faith is built upon, is calling to you now. Inviting you, begging you even, to spend time and enter the story that it may enter your heart and soul at their very core. It is a challenge and, like all challenges, will find us responding, reacting, resisting, seeking, hoping, searching, needing, wanting … that is relationship – that is faith.

What are we talking about then? In Liturgical Terms it is called 'The Triduum' and sees us journey through Holy Thursday, Good Friday, Holy Saturday and into the dawn of Easter Sunday with its emptied tomb and death conquered forever. It is a journey in faith, neither easy or fast but certainly rewarding. The potential is there for us to be moved to a place where we cannot but respond, to a point where our faith is revealed as central to all we are and all we seek to become – indeed to all we need to become.

In the pages that follow, we will look at the days of The

Triduum, examine some of the key moments in the Liturgies we celebrate and, God willing, in all that find something of God's will for us. These pages might well be a travelling companion for you as you follow his direction, hear again the message and seek, with the Universal Church, the peace that only he can give. You are as much a companion to others as they are to you – like the two men sent out together in search of a man carrying pitcher of water and not sure what or who they would meet. As it turned out, they found everything to be exactly as they had been told.

HOLY THURSDAY

While The Triduum begins with the Mass of The Lord's Supper on the evening of Holy Thursday there takes place, in many dioceses, a significant gathering earlier in the day. In some dioceses, for various reasons, this gathering might take place the previous evening or at another time near Easter. The gathering is for the Chrism Mass and sees the diocesan bishop gather with the priests and people of the diocese in the Cathedral to celebrate together the institution of the Priesthood and the blessing and consecration of the Sacred Oils of Catechumen, The Sick and Chrism to be used throughout the diocese in the coming year. At this Mass, the bishop speaks to the priests about their shared calling to be present to God's people in the diocese and during the Mass, priests of the diocese and resident in the diocese renew their commitment to priestly service. It is noteworthy that this is the only Mass celebrated in a diocese on Holy Thursday morning.

Later that same day ...

Did you ever think about the man carrying the pitcher of water in Mark 14:12–16? It would be a pity to overlook him on a day like today. We are not told much, indeed anything, about him as a person but he is a key figure. Jesus had told his disciples, 'You will see a man carrying a pitcher of water' and that they should follow him to the house where he was going. You would wonder about him. How many times he must have filled that pitcher, countless times in truth, and walked the street back to the house. That day was different though. His everyday task became a sign, a sacrament perhaps, and his role in this ever-unfolding drama took centre stage. He was noticed! There is something about noticing people, not least when they do not expect it, and it is linked with noticing the difference they make.

There is a story I like to tell, a moment I like to recall, when I waited for a friend outside Penn Station, New York. The place was busy, as you'd expect, with hundreds of people walking and talking. In the middle of Penn Plaza, I noticed pigeons pulling at a large piece of bread someone had dropped. Their work was continually interrupted by the passers-by and the pigeons flew to and from their find but were having very little success in taking any advantage of it.

I watched, maybe without even knowing I was watching, and then I noticed a man walking towards me. I would put him in his late twenties and a bit alternative perhaps! Black T-shirt, tattooed forehead, faded and torn jeans, a dangling earring and still a man who could blend into and get lost in the crowd. He walked through the pigeons and they scattered. Then it happened! He stopped and, as I watched, I saw him go back to the bread, go down on his knees and take the piece of bread in his hand and begin to break it into pieces. He rubbed the broken pieces on the ground and they became almost dust-like. As I watched, I thought his movements awkward and laboured but admired what he was doing. He got up, walked away and the birds flew back to the broken and scattered pieces. No longer were they congregated around one piece, now there was feeding to be done.

As he walked past me, I heard myself say 'Well done!' I don't know where it came from and neither did he. He stopped, and looked at me and asked 'What do you mean, "well done"?' 'That's a good thing you just did', I said. He smiled a little, looked at me and said, 'If I didn't do that, only the greedy ones would get it'. I was silent but filled with admiration and then I noticed, one of the arms of his T-shirt hung empty, he had one arm. I thought again about the awkwardness of his work and realised that, with one arm, he had done what I failed to do – notice, react, respond and make a difference. He walked away but his action and witness stayed with me.

'If I didn't do that, only the greedy ones would get it'. That is the line that stayed with me most I think. He was so right. It was, in truth, because bread was broken that it could be shared and shared generously with others. This takes us to the Upper Room where tonight's Liturgy has its birth, but we must not forget the man carrying the pitcher of water, no more than I must not forget the man on bended knees, one-handed, breaking the bread.

Holy Thursday calls us to a place of awareness around Eucharist and Service. These two are centre stage in all that is happening today. We are asked to be aware of people around us, to notice people, not just for the sake of noticing but because otherwise they might all too easily go unnoticed. The man with the pitcher of water had no idea where his daily task would take him and, not just him, but all who have come to hear his story right up to this present day, right up to you reading these words and wondering about Holy Thursday. That man is carrying the pitcher of water for you and me today, leading us down a street, to an open door and to an Upper Room where our place at the table is assured and the bread will be broken, divided, shared so that all, not just the greedy ones, may be nourished and uplifted so that like the pigeons we can take to the skies – where we are intended to be.

Eucharist and Service then are key to all we look for on this day. In this evening's Liturgy, there will be witness given to the Lord's call to be servants of one another. This, we are told, he did in the washing of his disciples' feet. They were reluctant to have this done, especially so Peter, who objected "'Never", he said "never shall you wash my feet'" (Jn 13:8). When Jesus pointed out that if he did not allow this to happen then Peter could have nothing to do with his ministry, he changed his mind saying; "'Then not only my feet but my head and my hands too'" (Jn 13:9) – that response, that change of attitude is perhaps central to our approach to a moment like this. The willingness to be open to a new message and take on a role not imagined is, at once, challenging and exciting.

Where did Jesus get the water to wash the disciples' feet? Certainly, it is possible that it is some of that same water carried by the man with the pitcher. That water too, finished up beside the wine on the table and may well have been mixed with it as we see time and time again when the bread and wine are offered at the altar. Noticing! That's the best gift you can bring to this day. Noticing! Noticing people, noticing signs, noticing what is done around the altar and noticing the people involved and those, like the man who carried the water, who may well be behind the scenes. Noticing!

Feet washed, and altar approached, we will hear again those words and see again those gestures first seen and heard in the Upper Room. Try, if you can at all, to locate yourself there in a place where you can see and hear. Observe the movements, the taking of chalice and paten, their being lifted/offered to the Heavens, so they can be shared with all around. See the man, on his knees, outside Penn Station, taking the bread and breaking it so that all would have a chance to be nourished, not just the strong or the greedy.

Notice the ending of Mass tonight. There will be no final blessing, the priest will leave the altar in silence with no closing hymn. He may well carry the Eucharist to an 'Altar of Repose' where adoration might continue for a number of hours but there is no formal ending or dismissal. This is because the prayer is truly only begun and will continue through Good Friday, Holy Saturday and all the way, to the discovery of the empty tomb on Easter Sunday morning. It is great that you are here. It is where you need to be and where you are needed.

Notice! You may well be carrying a pitcher of water. Someone may need to follow you.

SIGNS AND SYMBOLS TO NOTICE

✢ Church decorations such as bread and grapes, a white towel and basin. The tools of service.

✢ Return of the Trocaire Lenten Campaign boxes. A call to share.

✢ Ringing of the bell during the Gloria. It will not sound again until Easter.

✢ The empty Holy Water fonts. Dryness of spirit. Emptiness.

✢ Stripping of the altar after Holy Communion. No celebrations.

✢ No final blessing at Mass. A silent procession from the altar.

✢ A seamless prayer from Holy Thursday to the Easter Vigil/Sunday.

✢ Continuous prayer.

✢ A time for waiting and reflection.

✢ Procession to the Altar of Repose.

✢ Often a time for quiet prayer for a few hours into the night.

✢ Akin maybe to 'the wake' – being with and in silence.

✢ Silence! A time to reflect and anticipate the days to follow.

GOOD FRIDAY

Did you ever read the obituaries, maybe online or in the newspaper, or hear them on your local radio station? You learn of the death of someone you knew or had some connection with in the past. You begin to wonder should you go to the funeral. Then the questions begin. 'Do I need to go?' 'Would I be missed?' The mind is leaning towards 'no' but the heart is still tugging. There are many good reasons not to attend and yet, somewhere within, there is a feeling that it is the right thing to do.

Good Friday sometimes seems like that. There was a time when everything closed, even the television just displayed a test card or maybe a religious image and played music, but the regular programming was suspended for the day. Shops too and businesses all closed or at least closed in the afternoon to allow for attending at religious ceremonies. Of course, that has all changed but the reality of the day remains. This is the day Jesus died. This is the day he gave everything he had for us and somewhere there is a call going out to respect and respond to this hour.

So, do we decide to attend that funeral? Chances are we do and, even if it means changing plans, usually the feeling is of having done the right thing in attending. Maybe a family member looked at us or held our hand in a way that said; 'It means so much that you're here, thanks for coming'.

Make the decision then! Decide to attend the ceremonies in your parish on Good Friday or maybe to attend later in the day if work commitments won't allow for being there at 3pm. It is the decision to be there that matters, and what happens when you go is, in many ways, out of your hands. It is your gift to the ones being supported. Today it is your gift to the Lord. Rest assured, it is a gift that will be received with open arms – the outstretched arms on Calvary's cross.

It is a liturgically rich day. On entering the church, you may well stretch out your hand to the Holy Water font, only to find it empty. Waters will be blessed again at the Easter Vigil but, until then, the font is dry – a reminder that something very different is happening. You will notice the open and empty tabernacle (where space allows for reserving the Blessed Sacrament elsewhere) and again this is a reminder that Jesus' passion and death is being recalled and, without him, there is no Eucharistic celebration. The church will be sparse in it décor – no flowers, bright banners or sanctuary lamp. All pointing towards a sombre mood and the sharing of grief.

Today no music will be heard as the priest and ministers enter the church. In silence, the procession will go to the foot of the altar where the priest (dressed in red vestments) will prostrate – lie face down at that same hour Jesus 'gave up the Spirit' and died on the cross. On his ordination day too, the priest, lay flat like this while the church prayed for him in the Litany of The Saints. It is a sign of submission and of acknowledging the power of God's hand for us to find our feet and direction.

Today's Liturgy has three distinct parts:
(i) The Liturgy of the Word: this takes us through readings from the Old and New Testament that point to the why of our gathering today and to the proclamation of the account of the passion given in John's Gospel. You may well have the text in your hand but, in many ways, the words you read and hear today are words that are very familiar to you. Maybe listen and leave the reading until later. Listen for a phrase that you'd not noticed before – maybe Jesus' early question to the approaching guards, 'Who are you looking for?' (Jn 18:4). Peter's threefold denial (Jn 18:15–26) and with that, some thought around how we might do likewise. Hear the crowd chant 'Crucify him' (Jn 19:15) and reflect on how easy it is to get caught up in a mob culture. Left to ourselves, we would hardly shout for a man's death but when lost in the hostile crowd, the negative word can all too easily be found and heard from our lips. Keep an ear out for Pilate's 'Truth, what is that?' (Jn 18:38) or Jesus saying, 'I am thirsty' (Jn 19:28). If you can hear some of these lines today, rather than feel you must read them, it is likely they will sit more deeply with you. A lot will be said and there is a lot to listen to but maybe there is just a line, even a word, that is intended for you today. Just be open to it.

Alongside the reading of the Scriptures, this part of today's Liturgy includes some prayers for the world and its many needs. Prayers will be offered for religious and civil leaders, for those who have no faith, those who share other faiths, the Jewish people, those preparing for baptism and others. There is much emphasis placed on these prayers but, from your point of view, you are here to be part of the praying community. This is, in many ways, what you are bringing to this afternoon – a willingness to engage with faith and to be a key part of it through the sharing of prayer.

(ii) The Veneration of The Cross: a few years ago, a woman told me that she was going to the church on Good Friday and her young daughter asked her, 'Mammy, do you think I'll be able to reach the cross this year?' The mother was amazed by the question and then realised that her daughter had been by her side the year before but was not tall enough to kiss the cross. Reaching the cross has, I think, something to do with an awareness of its meaning in our lives. Chances are we are all reaching for it in some way or another – trying to understand more of it – some, sadly from the vantage point of the cross itself as they struggle with personal illness or the illness of a family member. The answer, we are called to believe, lies in some understanding of the cross and Jesus' triumph over suffering and pain.

The cross will be carried through the church and three times the priest will stop, hold the cross on high and say 'Behold the wood of the cross, on which hung the Saviour of the world' and the response comes back 'Come, let us worship' – again, in the crowd it can be easy to say that but when the saying is done, it is my choice. Will I leave the seat, walk to the cross and offer a sign of reverence?

It is a personal choice and a journey that only you and I can make in our own shoes. Are we big enough to reach the cross this year?

That really is why we gather, to behold the wood of the cross and feel again the love Christ showed for us when he stretched out his arms on that cross. It was not to be an end but a bridge and it is a bridge we all are called to cross, literally CROSS, in our lives.

(iii) The Distribution of Holy Communion: this reminds us that the Eucharist remains our strength and solace. It will be a very simple ceremony, with the taking of the Eucharist from its place of repose to the altar. There, the priest will call us to pray the Our Father. Holy Communion will then be distributed and, following a short time for private prayer, the afternoon's liturgy will conclude with a closing prayer. Again, the priest and ministers will leave the church in silence. Like Holy Thursday, this gathering is part of a continuing prayer and will reach its conclusion at the Easter Vigil.

Traditionally a collection is taken at the Good Friday gathering to support the upkeep of the Holy Places in the Holy Land. This is seen as a day when the Universal Church might support the Holy Land and the upkeep of the places associated with the life, death and resurrection of Christ.

SIGNS AND SYMBOLS TO NOTICE

✛ Empty Holy Water font – same as on Holy Thursday.
✛ Empty tabernacle, doors left open and sanctuary lamp quenched.
✛ The starkness of the church. It has little or no decoration.
✛ Symbols/Tools of The Passion:
  ✛ hammer, nails,
  ✛ blood-stained cloth,
  ✛ crown of thorns,
  ✛ vinegar/sponge.
✛ The colour of the Liturgical vestments: red, linked with sacrifice.
✛ The priest lying down in the sanctuary as a sign of submission to God's will.
✛ The telling of the story of Good Friday.
  ✛ Betrayal.
  ✛ Denial.
  ✛ False evidence.
  ✛ Hostile crowd.
  ✛ Weakness of leadership in the one judging.
  ✛ The words of Jesus.
✛ Carrying of the cross.
  ✛ Three stops along the way.
  ✛ Reminding of the three falls.
  ✛ Counter-balancing the three denials of Peter.
  ✛ One call to worship.
✛ Central place of Eucharist.
✛ Silent departure and continuing prayer.
✛ Notice as well the Stations of the Cross. Maybe take a look

at a few of them and offer a prayer for the people involved. Pilate and those in leadership that they have courage. Mary at the Fourth Station and a prayer for parents and family life. People battling addiction at the seventh station where Jesus falls the second time. Maybe just notice the Stations today and remind yourself that they are available to you all the time as opportunities to pray.

HOLY SATURDAY

This is in many ways, a day of mourning. Churches remain open, but the decorations are kept to a minimum with altars left bare, tabernacles left open and Holy Water fonts remaining dry. Mass in not celebrated during the day and Holy Communion may only be taken to the seriously ill and dying. It is also recommended that it be a day of fast, penance and reflection as we await the great news of resurrection and the empty tomb. It is a day to recall the ministry of Jesus and to ponder on a world without his saving presence and message. In our own terms, it might be likened to the day after the death of a loved one, when we try to come to terms with what has happened and give some thought to what our future might be like.

What can we bring to this day? Most likely the answer is found in remembering some of what has happened since Thursday. The Chrism Mass, The Mass of The Lord's Supper, the celebration of The Passion on Good Friday with our listening to the Scriptures as they open to us again the story and events of that first Good Friday, remembering our prayers for the world and its many peoples of all faiths and none. We might remember again our journey towards the 'wood of the cross' and our act of reverence there. We could spend some time around the moments leading to Jesus' death on the cross, the people he spoke with (Mary – his mother, John and the 'good' thief). We could well think about the hostility of some of the onlookers, the vinegar held to parched lips, the mocking and the humiliation of Jesus. We should recall the faithful friends who, even in silence, stood with and for Jesus. There were people like Joseph of Arimathea who wanted to bury Jesus' body with dignity and the women who noticed where he was buried so that they could come back and tend to his body in accordance with their tradition. A mix there, as everywhere, of people of good and bad intent. It is a day to align ourselves and recognise to which group we wish to belong.

There may well be value in trying to align our thoughts with those of the disciples, of Mary and the women who had accompanied Jesus and to wonder how they felt on the day we now recall. Did they see any hope? Had they forgotten his words and promise? Did they see this day as the end rather than a bridge? If we could begin to imagine the confusion, sadness, despair and for some perhaps regret experienced by those who knew him best and loved him most, it is likely we will come to a place of empathy where we feel the full impact of his death and dare to hope, to believe that there may be a future following on from and built on his Good Friday death.

It is a day to wonder and wander in faith.

THE EASTER VIGIL

The Easter Vigil could well be compared to the traditional wake. We gather to be with family and friends and to offer comfort to those who grieve the loss of a loved one. The 'wake' in its fullest form involved people gathering in the home of the deceased, spending time there – talking, praying, remembering and passing time in the company of a family in grief.

In its ideal setting the Easter Vigil would last for many hours. The beginning would be as dark descends and around a fire – a fire that dispels darkness and calls us to gather in its warmth. Here, some of the stories would be shared and the important events recalled. This would not be done in haste. Rather, there would be time given to this ritual of gathering. To this flame, we bring our hopes and dreams, our joys and regrets, our successes and failings, our holiness and our sinfulness.

Time, in many ways, is the key to the Easter Vigil and when followed as intended, a story unfolds and a sacred truth dawns. Indeed, it is to the dawn we are called during this special liturgy.

From a practical point of view, the Vigil is generally shortened in most parishes and includes the key elements but in a more condensed form. We will have the fire, and, in some parishes, it may well be outside and away from the church whereas, in others, it might be a simpler form of flame near the entrance to the church. The size and placement, though important, are not the key message being relayed. The symbolism of the fire – be it a large blaze or simple flame – remains that of being called to light. We might well remember here the exchanges between Peter and the three who linked him with Jesus, as they warmed themselves around the fire in the courtyard. There, Peter lost his nerve and denied Christ three times. There is choice for us too, at our own Easter Fire, to acclaim or deny, to walk towards or away but there is no denying the fire offers us an invitation to encounter.

You might remember the account of Jesus' death from Good Friday's reading of The Passion. At the moment of his death we are told 'The veil of the temple was torn in two from top to bottom' (Mt 27:51, Mk 15:38). At one level, this could refer to the awful sundering occasioned by death and of the often-irreversible breaking of the heart of those who grieve. It could be interpreted as a wound that can never be healed but there is a more comforting understanding of the veil's tearing. In the Jewish tradition, there hung a veil between people and the sanctuary and only very specific and chosen people were allowed view what lay beyond this veil. For everyone else, it was a barrier – physically standing between them and God. But now that 'barrier' has been torn in two and the sanctuary is open to all who choose to approach it. That's where we are at in the Easter Vigil – allowing the light to illuminate the sanctuary. It is not instant but rather the fruits of a spiritual journey. We are then, being invited to look not at a veil but what lies beyond it.

Again, you may well have a text in your hand for this evening's vigil but maybe we can just look at some of the moments you will witness and at some of the words you will hear. That way, maybe you will feel more at home with all that takes place since this is truly intended to be an experience rooted in family and in home.

The blessing of the fire is accompanied by prayer asking God's blessing and reminding all gathered that there is belief that we too can be 'inflamed' by our gathering to recall this sacred night.

The Easter or Paschal Candle is then blessed. Into its wax is traced the sign of the cross and at the top and bottom of that cross are the Greek letters 'Alpha' and 'Omega' – the first and last letters of its alphabet, symbolising Christ as 'The beginning and the end' of our salvation story. The current year is also inscribed on the Paschal Candle, situating us in time, in the storyline of our faith and reminding us also, as we will hear, 'that all time belongs to him and all ages'. We are literally putting where we are, here and now, in his care and under his guiding hand.

Five grains of incense are then pressed into the wax, reminding us of the five wounds on the body of Jesus, feet and hands pierced by nails and his side opened by the soldier's spear. The wax represents the body of Jesus and the grains pressed into that body, remind us of the suffering endured for our sake.

Fire and candle blessed, grains of incense inserted, the priest (deacon) lights the candle from the Easter Fire. The flame on the candle now takes centre stage and represents the Risen Christ, the light of our lives. From his light comes all light. The church is entered and three times the words 'The Light of Christ' will be spoken or sung and you, with all around you will respond, 'Thanks be to God'. These words are spoken at three different stages of the journey from the porch of the church to the altar. After the words are spoken for the second time (usually half way up the church), lights are taken from the Paschal Candle and passed to the candles held by the congregation. This is a powerful moment in the Easter Vigil when, from the one light – the Light of Christ – light spreads to and through those willing to accept and share it.

An Easter hymn 'The Exsultet' will either be sung or recited when the Paschal Candle is placed in its stand. 'The Exsultet' is a long hymn that tells of the wonder of this night and traces something of the history leading to it. Again, that notion of 'the wake' and memories being evoked. 'This is the night of which it is written: The night shall be as bright as the day, dazzling is the night to me, and full of gladness.' Again, in another place we will hear, 'We pray you that this candle, hallowed by the honour of your name, may persevere undimmed, to overcome the darkness of this night'. Just listen to the words and maybe you will hear something you need to hear this evening. Chances are you will not hear exactly what the person beside you hears and vice versa. This is fine, it is a personal encounter, so invite a word, a line or a phrase to take you to where you need to be brought this night.

The next part of the Easter Vigil introduces us to seven readings from the Old Testament and two from the New Testament. The Old Testament readings trace the story of our salvation and God's role in the world – from creation onwards and traces too how people lost faith in God, abandoned him and 'walked other ways'. In many cases all seven readings are not used but maybe three of them. Each reading will be followed by a prayer, drawn from the sentiments expressed in the reading. After the last reading concludes, the altar candles are lighted and the church lights come on. The Gloria will be said or sung and there will follow two readings from the New Testament. This reminds us again that Christ is the bridge between the Old and New Testament – in effect, the fulfilment of much of what is written in the Old Testament.

Later in the Vigil Easter water will be blessed and, in some cases, baptism may be celebrated. Where this happens, it will most likely be a baby or babies from your parish but, in some cases, adults who wish to be received into the Church may well be baptised at the Easter Vigil. Should this be the case, you will stand with them (and the infants being baptised) as a reminder that they are being welcomed into a family of faith. There will be a renewal of baptismal promises and, with all around you will reply 'I do', giving witness to your acceptance of the faith on this Easter night.

The remainder of the Easter Vigil will be the celebration of Eucharist. Gifts received, blessed, offered, consecrated and received. This celebration is possible because of all that has happened over the commemorated days of the Easter Triduum and you have been part of it. You are part of it.

SIGNS AND SYMBOLS TO NOTICE

- The darkness of the church. Without Christ we are in darkness.
- The Easter Fire … a flame to be blessed.
- The Paschal Candle.
    - Alpha and Omega, beginning and end.
    - Cross.
    - The year.
    - The grains of incense – five wounds.
- The call to recognise 'The Light of Christ'.
- The faith to respond 'Thanks be to God'.
- The spreading of light through the church as candle lights candle.
    - Remember where the light came from-the Paschal Candle.
    - Christ, the source of all light.
- Notice the lighting of church lights, candles on the altar.
    - Darkness yielding to light.
    - Night giving way to dawn.
- Flowers around the Altar. A sign of joy and celebration.
- Hear the bell rung during the Gloria that has been silent since the Mass of Holy Thursday.
- The blessing of Holy Water.
- Hear the 'I Do' when baptismal promises are renewed.
    - Notice your own 'I do'.
- When leaving the church notice again water in the Holy Water fonts.
    - 'He is risen'.

AN EASTER SUNDAY STORY

Archbishop Joe Cassidy (RIP), former Bishop of Clonfert and Archbishop of Tuam spoke once at an Easter Sunday Mass about his childhood days in his native Charlestown, County Mayo.

He said that as children they loved to go the cinema and it was truly an escape for them. To get money for the admission ticket, he said he used to bring jam jars back to the local shops, where a refund of a penny or two-pence would be received, depending on the size of the jar. He recalled one Saturday when he was two-pence short of the ticket price and that he searched for a jam jar but to no avail. Then he went to his mother's kitchen and noticed a jar there but it was half full. He took it from the press, knowing that if he could return it to the shop, he'd have enough money to go to the cinema with his friends.

Having looked at it for a while, he decided against bringing it to the shop and replaced it in his mother's kitchen cupboard. His reason for doing so was the point of his Easter Homily.

In his own words: 'I put it back in the cupboard because I realised it was no use to me unless it were empty'. Then he added 'And neither is the tomb'.

It had to be empty …

CONCLUSION

I met a man one time. He greeted me from a distance in a way I had not heard before, 'Hey Father, what's the good word?' I talked with him for a little while and he told me that he was Jewish. Later I mentioned this to someone and was told that it is a greeting commonly used by people of the Jewish faith. I liked it.

So having moved from Palm Sunday with its enthusiastic crowd, to the Upper Room of Holy Thursday, the courtroom of Good Friday and the borrowed tomb of Holy Saturday, be pleased with yourself – pleased that you walked with him, pleased that you allowed yourself be nourished with Eucharist and pleased that you had the faith to 'reach the cross' on Good Friday. There's a place for happiness as well, that you warmed yourself at the Easter Fire and welcomed the spreading of light shared from the Easter candle and that, in all that you were 'there'. Your presence brought much to the gathering and without you the congregation would have been impoverished.

Thank you for sharing these pages. Hopefully they have

accompanied you along the way as you journeyed through these days. They were never intended to be the full story of Holy Week but a reminder that you had already made your mind up to do the right thing and honour his memory.

What word or hope have you been able to take from these days? Hopefully there is something to be remembered from these days that may well sustain us in days to come.

So 'what's the good word?'

'He is not here, he is Risen.'

God Bless you and Happy Easter!

THEY WONDERED

*Who will
roll the stone away
they wondered
as they wandered
to the empty tomb.*

*Borrowed!
like so many other rooms;
the Bethlehem stable
the Upper Room
Martha and Mary's kitchen
where great things happened*

*welcome offered
food prepared and shared
lessons in listening
borrowed yes, but always
willing to repay*

*Repay!
every act of kindness
every word of encouragement
every step taken
every difference made*

*Made ...
the tomb was made by man
He was made of God.*

*The stone was rolled away.
He is risen.
Alleluia! Alleluia! Alleluia!*

Vincent Sherlock